AF156989

„How to become an

Earth-Angel"

[„Wie werde ich ein Erdenengel"

ISBN: 9 783 738 609 950 / German]

©Clarissa M. Seite

[Proofreading, September 2015 by

Christina Murphy

Thank you so much for your helping hand]

BLOG:

ClarissaSeite.Tumblr.com

www.theralupa.de

www.heil-verzeichnis.de

MEMBERSHIP:

DGH / VFP

GERMANY

Dear lovely persons and friends, lovely Kids … lovely creations of all types!

Actually, it is pretty easy to become an "Earth-Angle"! Probably you just ask how easy can I turn myself in an "Earth-angel"?

It is so easy to do and it is for sure:

Open your heart and let all the love come in, into your heart; breathe deeply in your organism and just imagine – just at this time, that all the angles ("Earth-Angel" - Archangels – Cherubins) and however they are called, with bright and just almost golden light are around you.

Every one of them, they are holding hands with each other and they are building a great immense circle of "love and light".

Natural circulation

And you, YOU (a God's child), you are in the middle of this holy spirit of light and energy and your are getting brighter with each breath – more and more!

All angles of the whole world and in the entire universe (and that's unknowing judge and just like in "Star trek"), remember the beginning, "infinite amplitudes", running to you and forming a big crowd just when you want them do to it and they will support you for this action, when you need this power to come out of your heart.

Now, take a deep breath! NOW!

Just at this time, you are probably asking yourself "and now", how I'm supposed to become an "Earth-Angle", what do I really have do to, am I good enough for this! Which rules do I have to follow and when am I considered as "good"?

Just be yourself

Let your heart tell you how to live and act just every day with a good conscience.

Walk through the world with open eyes and send "Light & Love"

How to do it is very easy:

Do you remember, when you were a baby and you saw the light of earth just in that moment you gave your first scream?

Probably not you think "no" in your first moment of reaction, but remember that … take a little time after and think it over and feel the warming tender of love that you received in this moment of birth.

All Angles (beings from heaven) they were here and gave you a blessing, warm and tender welcoming, because you are a wonder of nature. All came in and gave you a lovely welcoming to mother earth – YOU – earth-human-being from the universe, from the creator-energy from above.

Your mum, your dad or whatever they are (were) called here around you and they gave you all the love & light – shining brightly and tenderly in a pure way of sense, sense of life.

- **Believe**
- **Live**
- **Love**
- **Laugh**
- **YOU**

Return all the light into your environment and be "happy and lucky" – when you are doing it. This is the main order of an "Earth-Angle".

Use every day a little more of your joyful energy and let yourself go with this high energy and get even higher in the "frequency of healing" in you and around you.

You will probably be rewarded. You will get an immense value for fulfilling your order and your goal for you. It will be such a great prize for you and mother earth.

Peace of mind!

Peace of mind? That's something for R.I.P. – People in this world, who have gone already from us. What does it matter for us you might ask yourself about it eventually?

Yes, of course you might think, but that's truly the way in the first place. Peace of mind, it is what it's all about; you will take with you in first place! It doesn't matter who and when you will appear in public.

In this life or may be in the next following one, when your soul is ready for it.

You and your soul are just one united piece, here and just now you will accompany on your way of live (your order from above). Be sure!

What does it mean for every one of you?

Now, live your order, feel yourself and ask your heart with humility. What is your order from above to <u>act for mother's earth.</u>

Even now, at this time of high vibration (highest energy) and the opening fifth dimension or whatever it is called (merman – time - age), it is more important to go into the reflection of the "natures of lights" here on earth. Doing good with a lot of love – delivering all these goods to the humans with doing well every day!

- **BE**
- **Interest**
- **Earth-Angle**
- **YOU**

All the possessions, the "must haves" ,which you think you desperately need are just an illusion, a myth fallacy. A fallacy you think you can find some fulfillment!???

The universe has great abundance of "riches of all arts" in case for us. All riches of the world suppose to be for all of us - <u>but with care and respect:</u>

- **Feel**

- **Together**
- **Stay – to be around – to be there**
- **For each other**
- **Loving**

Love as the highest power of energy that we know and may feel.

Such an endless love, a horn of plenty filled up with "Richness and Luck".

It would be so nice, when people are with all beings – creatures, with us – with others and all together carry and share all this power of love with all – All in all together!

.

That would be such a nice and beautiful thought and a great approach to life, a true elixir full of treasure – riches that we own and truly to worth follow.

A simple but such a powerful tool called „ *LOVE* “.

- **Trust**
- **Pure**
- **Real**
- **Tangible**
- **Feelings**
- **Power / energy**
- **Elixir of life**

Now, take a white piece of paper "Din A 4 sheet" and write down your thoughts about the words above - what do you fell when you read them – what's important for you … write them on a piece of paper or much better in your own diary "Earth-Angle"! ;-)

You can also just buy a new book for this special moment with blank sheets just for your new way of life as an "Earth-Angle" or receive it as a present from a special person.

Just, like you prefer. Apropos – By the way, the wish to change your life or way in life just requires certain amount of time with ease and just choose very thoughtful what you want to change out of your special heart.

Take a deep breath in and out

Breathe all the love and the light in and all the old stuff – old thoughts / ballast from the past and just from today slowly out! Continue!

Seven time in and out.

Love – life – peace – heart

Ahhhh, ok, just reminding me of a important view.

In this way, it is very important to clean yourself daily – your thoughts – your action – when this impulse comes to you then it is an offer to do this – then it is your personal leader inside who tells you what is necessary to do or just it is time to clean your body with water

… or drink a clear glass of water

<u>A higher level of oscillation just requires attentiveness and care:</u>

Your hands or / and your thoughts are just enough for it. Just go there with your awareness whenever you feel like doing this.

Now, go there with your thoughts or / and your hands and place your hands on this position!

<u>Here are some applications for daily use:</u>

1. Chakra – Root chakra – RED (Sternum; just between your leg on the heights to the venus hill) Liquid Lava
Earth – Earth color (sludge – black, stone – deep tones (Monks – Zen – E-Moll) the seat of primal power / sexuality.

2. Chakra – Sacral chakra – ORANGE (coccyx; under the belly) – fruits like orange - the seat of the origin – thrive- multiply - nature – base chakra.

3. Chakra – Solar plexus- chakra – YELLOW (bellybutton – solar plexus) –spices like the spice of safran – The seat of soul / intuitive - let the sun rise.

4. Chakra – Heart chakra - GREEN (In the middle of the chest / thymus) -woods – lawn – the seat of Love / highest power.

5. Chakra – Throat chakra - BLUE (apple) -sky– air – wind – The seat of impression and communication / the door to heaven.

6. Chakra – Forehead chakra – PURPLE (In the middle of the forehead – between the eyebrows) the seat of the third eye. Soul watch – watch inside –clairvoyance – origin - intuitive.

7.Chakra – Crownchakra – VIOLETT / White (Head vertex / Medulla Oblongata; occiput /

troughout the neck / highest spirit /1000 foliage crown
The chakras are mainly – in the base, seven, but we have even more around us – behind your body, on the soil in front of.

Our aura is a natural protector and at least a meter or about 9 inches around us. Just a great protector!
If you want to know more about "chakras" then please you can search for it in the internet or in special book themes.

Perhaps a special book about it would be good to know and get more information which I wrote in the upper text.

Another way of learning and effective daily use; here are **following exercise:**

"Autogenous training in short ways"

Attention - Please read page 125!

1. Silence exercise:

„ I am completely quiet and completely relaxed." (6x)

2. Heavy exercise:

„My body is pleasantly heavy." (6x)

3. Warm up exercise:

„My body is pleasantly warm flowing, warm flowing." (6x)

4. **Breathe exercise:**

„I breathe calmly and pleasantly, in and out; it's breathing me." (6x)

5. **Heart exercise:**

„My heart beats calmly and regularly to the beat." (6x)

6. **Solar plexus:**

„My solar plexus is cozy & warm, pleasantly warm." (6x)

7.   Head exercise:

„My forehead is pleasantly cool"
(3x)

We always quite this relaxation exercise with the following ritual:

1.   Clench your fists. – 2. Bend and stretch your arms several times.

Please proceed do these following steps every day in the morning – in the afternoon, in the evening and at night time and you will be very successful

So, my butt is hurting so much now, because I'm sitting on my mother's old piano chair and I still don't understand how she could sit there for so long on this chair, while playing for hours on the piano! ;-)

But now, I have an information from above I should tell you, before I make a break.

For your child (Idigos of new age) or just for yourself I recommend the following activities:

Drawing / Mandalas
Music / Singing / Dancing / Jumping / Playing
Writing / Journal / Books / Lyrics / Blog
Playing games / Creativity
Reading / Earth-Angle-Story / Fairies / about God

Enjoy nature walk / Forest / Meadow / Water / Creek / River
Ocean – Mountain – Hill -
View points

Those elixirs are life of a special art!

We will learn again to get into contact with our own soul and we start living again with us and our soul! Then the higher beings / creatures speak to us with blessing words and holy energy.
Bring and turn your inner quality to the outside and let all human beings be part of this. Share your intra knowledge with all of them and let them have something from your energy - your higher spirit.

Teach your children, all kids, all friends – humans – people how to feel – how to taste – smell, see with open eyes – to listen – and all of these important qualities of humans; to be, to find yourself again and to get back to

... your soul!

Golden Rules

Here are some golden rules for daily use. Seven rules in a row for you for the daily routines with others. Take it and use it now:

- Smile every day a bit more
- Greetings to all humans around you
- Help other people, especially the older ones (crossing the street)
- Have an open ear for small-talk

- Offer you help to others or whatever is needed at that time in your environment.
- Never tolerate injustices; never! Send love & happiness; reach your hand, send hope and watch the sky and stars.

Sometimes we think, well, that is what I am already doing... Are you sure, all that is already flowing in your body and blood? Well, that is just wonderful and you have already been so far to be just the way you are now! **Congratulation!** You are in the process on becoming an "Earth-Angel".

Only God knows what is happening and has already been done or even not.

Who knows what the facts are and it is not that important and even not so important what other people think, think about you – what you do. It is more important how you will do it and how intensively you are acting in your job or life.

Do it and do it well!

It can only be guidelines or a manual for you, when you take all your <u>ownership</u> and give your doing and your living all the respect it needs.

Please remember it as long or as short it will be… every day is an important day, every day counts in your karma and determines your acting.

<u>Remember:</u>

Clean yourself - (Your soul)

Align yourself every day „new & positively" - (thoughts)
Breathe deeply in and out; evenly – (body)

Yes, it is also most important to note, that we are as an "Earth-Angle" normal human beings, who realize our action in a special way with high energy and our powerful and brightening action of doing.
The energy flows in our cannel throughout you! You are a carrier of this powerful energy and you have this power to act. Let it flow in your action to be. Use this power with smartness and found organizations about Conservation with Love and Peace and *be precious:*

Light carrier
Love carrier
Peace carrier

Live your life in order of an
"Earth-Angle" on earth, no
matter how or what you are;
the time is just now and it's
your time now to exist with
your way of living with love for
your mother earth – your
home!

- Herb-garden
- Fruits & vegetables
  perhaps on the roofs of
  buildings – Kindergar-
  tens – Schools – Bus
  stations – Homes –
  Houses
- Paint your area with
  colors / Street-Painting
  / Walls-Painting with a
  special message
  "God blesses you eve-
  ry day"

"Love is the answer" …
always…
"Peace on earth"
"Bread & water for all
creations on earth"

- Establish a club
  for your area
  with important
  themes like:

"What is the sense of
life"

"Sense of being great"

"Give & Take"

"Young & old"

"Walking-Club"

"Lucky & Healthy with
each other"

"Children care for Chil-
dren"

"Lucky Life Club"

"Together we are"

Powerful – strong – happy – important – peaceful

"Learn & Play"

"Be & Grow"

"Read & Write – Club" over Angle – Fairies – Dolphins – Unicorns – Loving (and walking into the future) with hope – faith – sharing!

More – More – More – More … you will – you can!

"Angles & Helpers"

I was pointed out, that Angles and Helpers are to be mentioned. I will try to do this and write it done, with the right meaning and grace. When you like it, you can call them!?

Remember:

You always carry the free will in you!
Your mind and your soul are free.

Archangel / Angels / holy beings / Masters call them just by the name, call it out loud or call them clearly or pray.

How?

Remember:

Dear Archangel Gabriel, help me by receiving healing / Decision / Journey / Learning and give me the right power and strengths. Deliver and clear me from negative energy and fill me up with refreshing and new energy!

Confusion / Disharmony / Structural loss
Friday / Root-Chakra / Red

<u>Dear Archangel Uriel,</u>
bring me peace and serenity; the inner peace and promote the brotherhood and sis- terhood in us, with us and around us. Please release me from the mental and emotional shackles and save me from all the greed, the origin of anxiety!

Fear / Greed / Rarapacity / Thursday / Solarplexus chakra / Yellow-Gold

<u>**Dear Archangel Chamuel,**</u> please forgive me, help me to forgive others too; to discover my compassion and my love in my heart. Help me to change all these negative feelings into positive emotions. Fill my heart with unconditional love!

Negativity / Heat / Pain/ Monday / Heart chakra / Green

<u>Dear Archangel Michael,</u> take care of me and send protection from all the evil; cut the strings / Entanglements of the past / now cut and relieve with your mighty sword. Return all force & power back to me!

Problems / Fear / Bad thoughts/ Threat / Tuesday / Throat chakra / Blue

Dear Archangel Raphael, please, I ask for concentration and direction. Show me the right way and let me see the divine plan. Also support me the way of Healing / Learning / Prosperity / Travel / Human support / Vision / Clairvoyance!

Darkness / Dead End / Pressure / Wednesday / Third Eye / Purple

Dear Achangel Jophiel, please let me find your enlightenment and that I find my light through with your help. This enlightenment will let me find the access to the great masters and their teachings.

Give me the power and the attention to align me to the light.

Please grant me the true knowledge!

Bigotry / Ignorance / False Pride / Sunday / Crown chakra / Violet

<u>Dear Archangel Zadkiel</u>, I beg whole-heartedly of valuable cleaning and conversion. Your assistance helps me to live more tolerance and forgiveness out of the deepest of my heart. You can only take all the pain, all the hardness all negative thinking, away from me and release it completely!

Entanglement / Narrowness / lower Energy Saturday / Soul chakra / White-Bright

And please, never think that it would be too much of asking for help!

No, never because angels are here, to spread happiness and they are so happy to help us and stand on our side to help you with positive power. This creates positive power.

Also you can listen to your heart and call the masters of the past or right here in time and ask for help when you need it most. They are here to help you all the time. Just open up your heart and with truly intentions you always be supported.

Even those Masters (your holy friends) will show you your way and all the options you will have or get.

Our friends the animals / power Animals Oracle / Tokin are here to help you to find you, your being and to get your inner power back.

The Dolphin / The Owl / The wolf / The Snake / The Raven...

Lovely Humans

Lovely Light Essence

Lovely "Earth - Angel"

Lovely Indigo & Lovely Children

<u>**You are the awaited for:**</u>

Hope

Confidence

Trust

New Age …

…   New Start

I would now love to present some of my favorites like "books & cards". I deeply recommend them and you can use it daily at your work as an "Earth - Angel" with or to get an advice or as a supporting tool.

Here are some of my favorites:

Books like:

Louise L. Hay / Healing for Body, Minde & Soul

Heart advice – your voice inside / Herzensweisheiten / Deine innere Stimme u. s. w

Amseln Grün / 50 Engel für das Jahr /
50 Engel für die Seele! u. s. w.

Armin Risi / Machtwechsel auf der
Erde und viele mehr / Unsichtbare
Welten

Susanne Hühn / Protecting Angels /
Schutzengel

Gondolino / Bücherschatz / Engelge-
schichten, die Kinder helfen

Jennie Harding / Chakren u. s. w

Glaser - Vogt / Reiki u. s. w.

Diana Cooper / Angels / Engelratge-
ber

Heidemarie H. Pielmeier / Tarot

Renate Anraths / Tarot – Dem Leben
in die Karten schauen

Michaela Fischer / Bewusstseins-
Wandel

Dalai Lama / C. Cutler

Jesus / Bibel

El Baba / …

Thorwald Dethlefsen / Erich von Däniken (Cods) / Hajo Banzhaf / Rüdiger Dalke / Tepperwein / Dan Millman (peaceful warrior – Numbers and so on) Stefanie Merges (Dreidimensional, Du bist mehr als du denkst) and so on.

Card Set:

Karten der Selbstheilung / Spezzano

Body & Soul - Körper und Seele / Louise Hay

Angel-Cards Engel-Karten / Diana Cooper

Der spirituelle Lebensratgebern / The spiritual way - Diana Cooper

Atlantis / Diana Cooper

Tarot-Karten / Rider / Miki Krefting ...thats how it began - so fing Alles an vor 25 Jahren

Tarot-Karten / Crowley / Gerd B. Ziegler / Mirror of soul

Kipperkarten / Regula Elisabeth Fiechter

Angel cards - Engelkarten / Pia Schneider – Ruth Kendell

Stonebook - Das kl. Heilsteinlexikon / Angela Gentner – Günter Hohenberger

Token - Kraft-Tier-Orakel / Jeanne Ruland – Murat Karcay`

Maria Magdalena / Jeanne Ruland – Marion Hellwig

Angel cards - Engeltherapieorakel / Doreen Virtue

Seelenapotheke / Hirschi – Troxler

Beziehungskiste / Hirschi – Troxler

Body & Soul - Körper & Seele / Louise Hay

My favorite healing stones to put on – wear – or just carry, are:

Amethyst – Turmalin – Citrin – Bluetopas - Blautopas – Moonstone - Mondstein – Bergkristall zum Aufladen der Steine / Sonne – Magnesit – Achate aller Art – Jaspis aller Art – Charneol – Türkis – Hämatitt zum Entladen der Steine / Wasser / Engelstein / Drusen aller Art / Amulett – „Äskulapstab with snake" (mit Schlange ist meine persönliche Lieblingskette als Heilerin).

Oh great, how wonderful it is, so many rich treasures to transfer from human to human; angel to angel.

I love it to use this *"helping tool"*, to get ones again inspired every time of using them.

Open
Inlets
Breathe
Open up
New ones
Get in to it
Open up your heart and wide and let the love come in
Breathe deeply in and out with joy and happiness!

My lovely "Earth – Angel", now I truly hope, that I could show you the direction a little; the way to follow perhaps a little bit to get into. <u>You decide!</u>

Absolutely, I want you to rec-ommend to walk the **"Jacobsway in Spain"** or in another country to walk for a

while or even next door to you;
in your country to follow.

It might be a great idea.
It could be an asset for you.

And last but not least …

Please!

- Write a journal and put your dreams on paper and find out about the meaning in good books. Find out, what the soul wants to tell you.

- Reflection in a group or in a group of like mind-ed soul -sisters and brothers.

- Reading

- Writing

- Music

- Sing

- Dance

- Visit a theater or act in a theater

- Painting

- Crafts

- Knitting

- Writing as an actor

- Communication

- Laugh

- Be Happy
- Cleaning Rituals

And anything else you like to do…special…

And remember, everyone <u>is responsible for themselves and performs and live automatically the Healer – Code of honour (Codex)</u> with itself and with others. That goes without saying. <u>That's for sure!</u>

What does „Codex"(Code of honour) mean?

When you wish an energy exchange, it is normally carried out on the basis of natural or on the basis of commercial practices in the western world of money!

<u>Possible design of a meeting fee:</u>

One hour = 60 Euro, but not longer till one hour and a half = 80 Euro.

A fair design of commercial practices and usual local facts and circumstance is needless to say!

As an **"Earth-Angel"** you take action in the name of the „**universal energy**" and a compensation is always wished with fullest "joy and love".

Act and practice to the best of your "knowledge and belief" …

Love is the answer – always!

What do you think about it … write me, if you want …

"Love & Light"

Human!

You as an „Earth – Angel" … direct your way of doing ….

- As the saying goes ... do it and do well!

There is so much, what we can do for us, as to be well balanced and in the right measure.

- **As a balanced scale**

Also they're a lot of relaxation techniques offered and great rituals are available as well

- **But**

What does really fit to us and will be the right one at the end?

For one or the other it is perhaps "Yoga" for sure and the other one is "Zen-Practice" the best or even just reading a book about angels from Amseln

Grün or – Diana Cooper might be the right one?

Good, as well, but …

How about taking some little things in our lives (maybe with breathing) and we live it just like:

Love

Peace

Silence

Attentiveness

With each other

Then we have found and won a lot already – I think so!?

Every human and expectant "Earth - Angle" can decide what is good for him - her - his action and act as one.

How about having ... a beginning as:

I walk, when I walk

I sit, when I sit

I speak, when I speak

I cook, when I cook

I sleep, when I sleep

And so on....

... Without distraction in the

„here & now"

... with complete "awareness"!!!

Then you have, I believe, you gained much for yourself and for your "to be here " you won a lot ...

A good thing (Ritual), I believe, would be simply praying:

For me is praying at night a real good thing … sometimes I revel in my intentions … or sometimes on demand or desire… depending on your mood.

- Praying is a very good thing to clear your mind…
- Praying helps to get clear in your options
- Praying calms you down and brings you "comfort & peace"
- Praying above to the spiritual world / to God / to the masters or whatever will give you the right "power & strengths" to go on

The belief in goodness
in

"You"

&

the world.

A good thing would be to do some more rituals:

For me it has been:

lighting a candle because it proved …your matter … perhaps … more…

If it is possible then light a fire or a fire ritual at a decorated fireplace.

- In the light, I find a warm light dispenser
- The light is not only heat but also a cozy atmosphere
- In the light, looking into it and diving into the depths of thoughts, you can wonderfully "relax & dream"
- In the light, deep thoughts can be designed and created. They take shape and become reality
- In the light, things become clearer and can now be designed and are added into the heart.
- In the light, I'm aware of …

- In the light I find solace. It illuminates all the shadows in me and around me.

Another good thing would be to clean with warm & cold water – yourself, your whole body & soul

- The warm and cold water helps me and you to clarify
- To say goodbye to the old, used and to adopt eye sparked
- To let the old energy go and to take new energy up
- The cleaning lets you re- radiate back
- Hale and hearty start the day and usher the evening
- After every session you clean your hands with cold or warm water. Let old energy go and let new – fresh one flow in your system.

!I am a clean, bright and healthy light!

- Be good to yourself, treat yourself with good nutritious food and be as honest as possible and work with a clear conscience for a good cause
- Stand up, for you and justice
- Open up your heart for the good in you and the other essences of planet earth

! Believe with the fullest of your heart in yourself!

- Watch – be attentive
- Respect – even the othersness
- Love – without expecting
- Give - in accordance with taking
- Live – here & now

!I am happy – satisfied & heal - healthy!

!The Universe always provides me with „everything"

I am protected … always! …

My Arch-Angel – Masters – Helpers – high spiritual world are always on my side to protect me

I am clear in mind, honest and with pure heart …

My Angel helping me with … I pray with daily intense for me and for the world …

"LOVE & PEACE"

The universal power is big – great and full of "Love and Light"

„The route is the goal" - Konfuzius

You might now it from the newspaper; the little ads with "love-advice" and the sweet little figures from a man and woman ….

Love is …

Yes, what about … fall in love ….
„LOVE".

„LOVE"

„To love myself ... love … lovely …
sweet – loveliest - not"

I love you!?

Why – whatever – wherever – why - I
love you! … not?

AND

<u>I Love !?</u>

How –where – what … and why … I
love me! … ?

<u>Love is:</u>

Easy

Creative

Wonderful

Butterflies in the bellybutton

Heart beating bum bum bum

Jubilant

- - - - - - -

Heavy

Empty

Pressure

Dizzy

Bellyache … I feel sick

What about with that „Love" and how
do I love the best …?

That is the question; is that the question „per se" …

Love yourself with all your sides (Light
& Shadow) and you can love everybody just how he – she - is…

…

Unconditional love; without expectation neither on you and the other!

How I will handle myself; am I easy to handle or can I let myself be as I am!

„I am „mindful and respectful" and full with love to myself"!

And of course to all others "polarity law of attraction".

„I love me – I love you too"

I love you – me – the world – the nature – the animals – the plants – the forest – the water – the stones – the earth.

HOW?

This would be a wonderful way to give yourself and the other creatures just <u>love:</u>

- I'm loving me and realize / recognize my needs I desires
- I live a respectful life together with me and around me
- I show respect to the nature – the animals – the plants – the earth as well
- I give and take in unison; in moderation
- I recognize myself, even with all the different sides of myself
- I enjoy in moderation (eating – drinking – physical desire at all)

I bless all things around me and see what happens:

Example: I bless my food and drinks with positive energy (thoughts)

- I bless my body
- I bless my health
- I bless my doing

- I bless my partnership
- I bless my interpersonal relationships

- I bless the nature / the tree / the plants / the food
- I bless the animals / the food
- I bless the humans / the healthcare / the love
- I bless my thoughts
- I bless all my actions

Possible Affirmation:

I love myself like I am and all others around me too!

I open my arms very wide and tell the world:

„I let the love flow into my heart"

„ I bless you all with my love"

„My positive thoughts increase; the vibration of love"!

„I am – I am"

!NOW!

Just try it now:

- Breathe deep with fully re-spect, the love fullest love „in & out" …
- Again and again, as often as I think o fit … 3x daily…
- I hug myself lovingly / affec-tionately and I hug the world … 3x daily…

Breathe deeply in and out ...in the rhythm of your heart …

When Ideas come to your mind, just write it down ... and work on the dark thoughts … clear them … breathe love in your "Heart-Chakra" and change them with positive thoughts, then you are a **"God's Child"** and you are **always loved!**

Breathe deeply again into your heart and become "soft and wide" … so you and your thoughts become <u>soft and wide!</u>

Try it every day and watch your thoughts – watch your body and your connected soul … what is it doing with?

Write this down in your personal book and just when you want to do it; just do write down, what comes to your mind in this moment.

Feel the power (in you) and fill it in all your cells (Visualize your body and your inner life) with power and the great light "THE LOVE".

Feel and fill your cells and what the flow is doing to and with you.

Love as the highest goal; full with respect – mindfulness – commonality. Together and for each other, responsible for you reactions and your (well-) being!

My personal beliefs ... and what about yours?

- Open your heart and let the magic flow
- In your system down and up again ... let the love flow
- Can you feel the energy flow, nice and comfortable
- Love is the answer ... always
- Love is so powerful; it can save the world with this great power!
- Take your time
- Breathe deeply in and out /
- Breathe softly deep in & out
- When you get warmed up & you feel the silence, then you are doing very well with it.
- You are safe
- You are doing just fine
- You're safe, where ever you will go
- The way is the end & the start at the same time!

- And if the world comes, I plant another apple tree – Charlie Chaplin
- What can I do, to become a great "Earth-Angle"?
  … go on for five minutes and follow your personal goal and write down five ways.
- Every day, I'm willing, to learn a couple of new things in my life <u>like:</u>

  - Smiling
  - Laughing
  - Giving away some things
  - Being graceful
  - Loving
  - Sharing

<u>**Watching movies like:**</u>

  - The little Buddha

- The trip to the next dimension – (Die Reise in die nächste Dimension) – Clemens Cuba
- The peaceful warrior (Der friedvolle Krieger)– Dan Millman
- Healing (Heilung)
- Secret
- The secret of Celestine (Das Geheimnis der Celestine)

I create my personal collage with pictures and dreams / hopes / wishes / goals, which I like to reach!

I love to read books about:

Jesus

Dalai Lama

Gandhi

El Baba

Louise Hay

Angel's stories

Thith Nan Han

Amseln Grün

So much to discover …

read – read – read

write – write – write

- o Do
- o Be
- o Share
- o Give
- o Take
- o Believe

**There are so many motivational
cards from different teachers like:**

- Tarot
- Angel
- Runes
- Motivation
- And so on .

Use them and have fun with them!

Go and play and find out …

Three times a day:

Open your arms and let all the love flow into your body and mind.

Breathe deeply in & out …

Three times!

My favorite are:

Tarot card #14 (Flow / Give and Take in balance) and #21 (The world / Dance / In balance with yourself)

Healing stones are:

Rose quartz, tourmaline, citrine, moonstone
Blue topaz, rock crystal, onyx, Hypersthen

My vision:

The whole world stands on Mother Earth and hold hands „ We are all together their"

In Love & Peace!

New regulation from believes – action – live – being

All together in:

Love – Light – Peace

„Self – confidence"!

„Self – confi – dence"

I am self confident! – ! "I am "… Being with me ….

I am self confident! – I am …with me!

I am confident in being … I live self confidence in me and with **myself!**

I am confident with what I am feeling-thinking -

Acting according to my consciousness!

As I feel I react well – according to my "consciousness".

I know consciously what I want …

I feel what I think and I think with my feelings here and now – to BE

I'm aware of!?

- According to myself – confidence, I know who I am …
- I know what I am worth and I am aware of.

- Myself exactly knows, what it wants and I take me as I am.

- Fully – here and now – con-scious in myself in here / this.

I love myself as I am … with all my corners and edges … with all my shadows and I let a lot of light shine in me, full self respect towards me and deliberately even in here / this.

I am mindful – respectful and of fullest of love with me….

… Self-confidence

I will be careful with me and I let the criticism of me and others. I am a child of god – the universal energy!

Filling with

„Light & Love"

And with

„Self-confidence"

Forgiveness (tender and full of mind-fulness)

- A powerful instrument of the heart

How do I live, how can I implement forgiveness in my life.

What does it mean…" I forgive my neighbor and myself"

But I ask … but how?

- What comes to mind again and again and I think, not easy to implement, is how to forgive somebody…

This someone has…

Hurt me

Criticize me

Reprimand me

Slander me

Left me

Humiliate me

- Also we carry from year to year all this past deeds with us around, and also we have

committed themselves and
feel guilty for!?

Is forgiveness essential?

Where do I profit?

I want to express my anger and return
it to the other what he / she did to me.
Every day I blame myself for my action and feel bad about it.

I think and believe, that forgiveness is
a very important building block for our

"Being"

Who loves forgives!

- Yourself and believing on the
  good in you and others will be
  nourished and strengthened.
  To an extent which is often in
  the first not available (feel or
  see) but in the second you will
  feel in your feelings and see in

your extent how it will grow up
to something big!

How?:

- When I forgive myself primarily
  self and automatically the others with all their self-doubt and
  lack of self-worth (often you
  will find this there) forgive too,
  then I automatically create
  more & more of …

„Light & Love"

- For me and all the others on
  mother's earth.

Listen:

Forgiveness <u>does not mean</u> yes, of
course. I do not tolerate what others
do and how they treat everything else
…

No, that is not what I am doing with!

I release the feeling of heaviness free!

I free myself of the burden of dept

I free myself from the burden of guilt; the resulting atonement

I free myself from victimization

I free myself from the offender exist-ence

I free myself from bad opinions

I free myself of past being and I cre-ate me as a person and my con-sciousness completely new

I live freely and in LOVE!

Now, how can put (turn) this forgiveness into practice.

What else you could do

- Breathe deeply in your heart and write down all the wounded feelings and / or your doing
- Breathe deeply in your heart and spread your arms and let all the love come into your heart
- Let the current pain and thoughts come to the surface
- Breathe deeply in and out … several times … in and out until your trembling heart will not tremble so much anymore

- Fill your thoughts with words…
I… (Name) forgive myself and (Name of offender / victim) whole heartedly
I am so terribly sorry what happened between us … and I call the "universal power" (angel – helpers – holy masters) to free myself from that difficult situation / process / ritual to clean my heart and set it free, so I can gain strength from all the universal love!

I solve the black spots (symbolic clean up with a cleaning rag / scrape away with a spatula / purple flame) by cleaning

- I breathe deeply (new own comes in) and breathe with slow breathe (old one gets out) everything old / used up out
- After I freed myself and feel free (if not, just repeat the exercise several times a day or over the weeks - it will get easier from time to time) take a piece of paper, burn it or discard it, just how you like
- Pack your sheet of paper symbolically in a bag, lay it down on a boat and then let it flow away down the river.
- This would be another alternative. You can do it by thoughts. You can do this at any time of the day.
- I open my arms widely and spread them like wings and let the love and light come into my heart „ I open my heart for all the love" three times , daily

I am „happy and blessed"

Life gives me everything I need, what
I really need

Many thanks!

Thanks also all the angels – helpers
and universal energy as much as
YOU can

From being to being

Together – for each other – being
there sharing

Everything is a give & take!

Let us be there „for each other"!

Especially in today's fast paced global world, it is not easy to concentrate on the essential – the real thing.

The reason for this is really easy to explain.

Social networks and our very important smart phone (?), which we carry already to the breakfast table and also the very important computer and the commercial posters on the way to work do their best, to take our precious time and help us to get irritated. ;-)

Later in the late afternoon, a lot of people do a little surfing in social networks or "google" (twitter – facebook instagram and such) and then lay down pretty fast onto the coach or what else we get to grip like notebook or tablet or whatever is easy to reach.

Why do we function like that as a human being, in complete distraction!? Far away from the essential?! Away from the hot shot or whatever has been essentially important in the past?

The board game evenings are definitely over … every living person in the west has an electro vacuum , I call it like this because (computer – iPhone – iPod – smart phone - tablet whatever) they are present in every room.

The nightly walk to a device (is carried out) acts almost trance-like … like on a dead walk without any meaning and content!

Why? Do we need this … really!?

Is that the future we really want with each other or just to say - living side by side without recognizing the other soul …

Why does this happen with us human !?

Why do we run so fast from "A to B" and make a sprint in the hamster wheel until we collapse / burned out!?

What and are moves us to this state?

Why are we doing this?

Does it really make fun ?

Is that <u>really</u> desirable?

<u>Now! Listen! Look at this human!</u>

<u>Is this really useful – does it make any Sense???</u>

Why – why – why – why …???

Does it maintain our life … in a way as a "social essence"? Life well and long lasting ***"happy and satisfied"!***

Or is the way of sharing with each other just the happier and healthier way … ?

I think that we could recourse even more often to the traditional evenings like:

- Woman evening with women
- Men evening with men
- Pubs
- Dancing
- Cinema
- Just going for a walk
- Singing
- Playing cards
- Friend's evenings
- Coffee afternoons
- Crafts
- Do pottery

That could be very nice…

And if you can't find anything out of this list, finally go into a „club"!

- Date Club
- Bowling Club
- Tennis Club

- Saunas Club
- Swimming Club
- Soccer Team
- Sing Club
- Fly Club
- Foto Club

And what else could you find
to do.
And when this does not help
or it is not of your kind.
Go to a single dating or whatever.

.

You're right!

Humans are not always in the
mood or have time to do all
this…
TRUE!

At least it would be a good mix
to begin

Once a week or twice a month,

- away from all this elec-
  tronic stuff
- away from the chained
  habit.

Jump up and get out of the
house – get some fresh air
and get joy of more

Just try it and gain some more
with each other full of

- Happyness
- Joy
- Laugh
- Joking
- Other perspectives
- New friends
- New with each other

In this sense …

„It's not yet fall a master from the sky"

(Perhaps Jesus or some other holy masters!?)

Why always does this claim in yourself?

You have to be better than others…..

Why actually?

Do we had to feel or hear this at the age of a kid (child) by possible.

The:

- parents
- grandparents
- teachers
- sisters
- or from friends …

  I am better than you?

You are better then me?

Why is this that way …

Does man always seek for …

… more - more - more … more:

- Perfection
- Perfectionism
- Self – esteem
- Attention
- Respect

What is man about and how can I …

In order to find out, it would be an opportunity to realize what you like on yourself by taking off some time and taking a piece of paper and write down what you really like….

My personal examples:

I am good I am good I am good in:

- listening

- writing
- drawing
- comforting
- laughing
- shopping
- relaxing / watching

Find your own abilities / benefits / talents (in your relationships and in yourself) and write it down on a piece of a colored paper.

What I like about myself and what others like me / appreciate it:

If you do not know anything about it at this very moment, it's simple and easy; just ask your fellow human being in your personal environment area:

My abilities / benefits / talents:

Make yourself a list, what who when told and read, to you again and again.

Keep you loved it (List) one in a treasure chest or similar.

- That's you in a special way
- Nobody can take it away from you
- This you are is how you are from another perspective.
- You're in a different viewpoint
- You're treasure (In & Out)

Well, what is your opinion towards you – mean for you….

What does your „Self-Worth", how your self-esteem formed about?

- **Great**
- **Mittel**
- **Little**

<u>HOW – choose … it's your turn…</u>

What can I do, to make my self-worth work and that I feel comfortable -"I" feel comfortable…?

Exercise every day a little … stay in front of the mirror with a dog / cat / children / friend – friends

- WHAT
- HOW
- WHY
- WHO
- WHAT

Characteristics examples from my perspective:

I am beautiful, because God created me that way / and I have created me that way over the time…

I am talented, because my grandparents – mother – my father have given me this talent.

I am funny, because in my family have always been so funny.

What are your personal examples?:

What can I do to treat myself, my body – soul – spirit, to create and get something better … more beautiful … create something more blessing …

- body sensation
- thoughts
- well - being
- sport
- reading
- time

I am creating my self-worth and, I give myself all the love I need, respect for me and my body / soul / spirit by care and mindfulness:

- Because I love me

- Because I respect myself
- Because I will take proper care of me
- Because I grant myself self-worth

I like myself

I am happy with myself

I love myself

I am great, like I am

I am a likeable person – I am fine like
I am

I am – I am

I am a teacher

and

also

I am a student

always and again!

TIME

I have time …

I do not have time

I would like to have some more time

Time, what is that

My time is over

If I just had time … 48 hours a day …
then …

A lot of people wonder:

- What is the meaning of time
- What is time
- What is the value of time
- How can I create my time use-
  fully
- How do I use

I often hear statements like:

- Time is precious
- Time is money
- Time is gold
- Time is life
- Time is precious!

- Time is running out
- Time is rare
- Time is over
- Time is lost
- My Time is … over

What am I doing with my time

How, do I use my time

How do I create this…

precious time whisely

If I would have some time again …
then … I would …for sure … ;-)

- Travel
- Dance
- Listen to some special music
- And so much more
- What!

I have worked my whole life and I was successful (whatever you did) in my doing and still I miss …

What do you miss in your life?

What are your spontaneous responses to?

What comes into your mind?

How would you like to be… when

What can you change

Which things can you change possibly here and now…?

How you work on a small scale (first step) to reach the actual target?

Change – now – begin – do it – now – a new – design your time – let it go – loosen old rigid patterns.

By starting <u>now</u> you can change things.

HOW

!NOW!

Start to begin

One step after another

Structure a new yourself

!NOW!

You want some more time ….

Very easy

Take your time… !NOW!

 HOW … !NOW!

By omitting unimportant things!

Or rather „Old one out and new one in" …

…focused and reduced to the essential (ZEN)

- Time for the family/ husband/ wife/ partner/ women/ children / friends

- Get rid of your old stuff like clothes – overcome (structures) must go!

- Superficial so-called acquaintances (if they don't fell right anymore) let them go

- Superfluous furniture get rid of them and remove them from your flat

- Books you don't read anymore – OUT

- Buy good natural food for one day or maximum two days) Less shopping pressure – create more shopping experience)

- Hobbies "yes" of course but not too many - I now a lot of fellows

- Get more space and have more time

- Create a mediocrity / uniformity

- Create a good balance between give and take (with friends / work/family / time for yourself)

Make space for „NEW THINGS" &
make space for precious time!!!

Tick – Tack – Tick – Tack

You can never turn time back

Lost time is lost (time)

But, every day is a new day

<u>Begin – Start</u>

!NOW!

Grief / Despair / Pain

When your heart is tired

When your heart is heavy

When your heart is so upset

The deep pain in your bones; sitting in the body system and procured in various ways expresses

Why?

What happened – (what occurred), that you feel this way?

- Abandoned
- Been cheated
- Been lied to
- Charged – overloaded – overwhelmed
- Broken objects – lost items
- Ill
- Loss of a loved one

- Loss of a loved creature / animal

What <u>troubles you</u> and how can you <u>release</u> (process) it over the time!

What does it mean to release… growing - transformation?

From a time to time, it is important, to look at the things some time, thereby learn how to transform (Growth: feel by experience – feel – learn – "grow-out" of old / past and into the new (new ways))

Only then after time of realizing, able to accept, then can I likely release!?

You personally decide, when the time is right and how the situation will develop.

- Now, write down on a piece of paper, what's bothering you!?

On the second piece of paper you write down, how to release (process) and how much time you need, to let your sorrow go!

On the third piece of paper you decide which way your process goes now and what you have personally learned and what you will take from now on into the "new".

Leave yourself time <u>and feel</u> into your heart!

Only then

Let go

In

Love

Now I am cured and healthy

!NOW!

Exercise:

Put both hands on your heart (Heart - space) and breathe several times in … until you get very silent.

Visualize - Violet light of cleaning in your body – body cells – into the organs – in your bloodstream and say inside of yourself or clearly to hear …

"I am full of light and love – I am lucky – I am healthy and healed"

Every day I feel in every respect better and better!

Exercise every day in the morning – afternoon – evening – at night and whenever you have time. Treat myself every day to something good!

Quotes – My favorite <u>quotes and love affirmations are:</u>

The route is the goal! (my personal slogan)

[Konfuzius]

I know, that I know nothing (always remember the picture of Albert Einstein – as he shows his tongue)

[Albert Einstein]

Do not walk behind the past and do not look into the future.

Life is here and now!

[Buddha]

Love your neighbor as thyself!

(My favorite)

[Jesus]

I give you a new commandment: Love each other. You shall love each other; as I have loved you.

(Johannes 13,34)

The one of you is without sin, should be the first to throw a stone at her.
(My mum's saying)

(Johannes 8,7)

By loving forces wonderfully sheltered.
We are awaiting fearlessly what comes.
God is with us at dusk and in the morning
and most assuredly on every day.

 [Dietrich Bonhoeffer]

(Dietrich Bonhoeffer is my role model)

You have to wander through the night,
if you want to see the dawn.

[Khalil Gibran]

The planet doesn't need successful
humans anymore. The planet needs
urgent peacemaker – healer – reno-
vator – storyteller and lovers of kinds.

[Dalai Lama]

(One of my spiritual role model – my
holy friend)

Life of all kinds, whether they are human, animals or other, is precious and
they all have the rights to be happy.
Everything, what our planet popu-
lates, the birds & all the wild animals
are our companions. They are a part
of the world we share the world with
them.

[Dalai Lama]

We scare about our own sins, if we see it on others.

[Johann Wolfgang von Goethe]

Everything, what you can see, has its roots in the unseen world. It may change the form, but the essence remains the same.

[Rumi, the song from love]

The precious legacy of a person is the trace his / her love has left in our hearts!

[Vinzens Erath]

I open my arms widely and send:

"Love & Light"

To mother earth and into the infinite
universe beyond – !Now!

Every day again – new … every day
is a new day!

Do it and do it well; everyday again –
and again!

Love is the answer! Always!

<u>**Favorite Affirmation:**</u>

I am happy – save and sound

I am successful

I am completely healthy

I am …. [Louise Hay]

Everything is well laid out in my world;
everything is well!

I am „LOVE"

I fill every day with love and light; with
only one breathe!

!NOW!

(take a deep breath and fill all body
cells – bloodstream - organs)

 [Clarissa M. Seite]

We are filled with love and justice with
us!

Might the angels accompany with…

Mindfulness

Respect

Care

Love

Light

Get the power of LOVE

Get back the pieces of your lost soul

<u>**Get back – YOU!**</u>

<u>Sincerely Claire</u>

Table of contents

Personal Facts:

- First name: Clarissa M.
- Past name: Seite
- Praxis of Psychotherapy
- Mediumistic medial counselling
- Born: 19. August 1969
- Star sign: Leo
- Female
- Married

Contact:

- Road: Winibaldstr. 14
- Cip code: 82515
- Wolfratshausen
- Germany
- Webpage
  http://www.theralupa.de
  www.heil-verzeichnis.de

About me:

Clarissa M. Seite

Praxis for Psychotherapy

Naturopath of Psychotherapy

Mediale – psychological counselling

Psychological counselling –
Cards also on the phone

First Contact

 01525 - 654 99 30

www.theralupa.de

www.heil-verzeichnis.de

BLOG:
ClarissaSeite.Tumblr.com

REIKI – Master & Teacher

Addiction treatment

Maidname: Zickler

Born at:

19 th August 1969

Bad Neustadt a. d. Saale

Schooleducation:

Qualifizierenden
Hauptschulabschluss / GLSE

High -School in Louisiana /
U.S.A (Realschulabschluss)

University of Tech in Louisiana
One semester in Math – Art –
Science & English

Workeducation:

Saleswoman - Clerk – Insur-
ance Clerk – Naturopaths for
Psychotherapy – addiction
Treatment – REIKI-Master /
Teacher

Grown up in Speichersdorf near Bayreuth (Home town of WAGNER - Festival) until the age of 18.

Louisiana / U.S.A until the age of 21.

Germany / Bayreuth for one year in 1991 - Munich four years - Bayreuth 16 years – and Munich / Wolfratshausen since 2011

Till now:

Third marriage and two kids (one of the second marriage in 1997 and my step son from the third marriage in 2012 ;-)

- **My spiritual way …**

  began with the holy angels from my grandmother. I love them since I was a little child.

  I feel deeply in love with the angels and they are my special friends and I feel very close to them. In my childhood, my grandmother was always (every day) praying in church above to them. She (Anne – Maria Müller) was always talking about them with a smile on her lips.

The Angels are my deepest friends ever in closeness and deep love!

I got two special paintings from grandparents hanging in my living - room above my coach. Also I drew a lot of paintings about myself … they are everyway in my apartment.

At 1992 after I got divorced from my first husband Mike, I started with my first Tarot Cards from Mrs. Miki Krefting from Munich.

Many hours of learning – self teaching – many days and night of study and spiritual work on my intuitive work and gaining on spiritual power past by.

More and more of interest on themes like religion – Jesus – God – holy master like Dalai Lama and the universal power and the work with Tarot (Golden Raider) – Angels (Cooper / Virtue) and the Numerology (Dan Millman) – Dreams (C. Jung)– Astrology and many books of Louise L. Hay and others good literature to read made me grow to a good intuitive personality with a good profile over the last 20 years.

Kinesiology - TCM - Herbs – Homeopathy – universal energy of REIKI – and the birth of my special son Frank (Indigo) in 1997 have given me so much universal power to share with human – friends – in my family – with other people around me!

2008, after ten years of study, and practice in the spiritual world with a lot of „doing and learning" I finally began to study naturopath of psycho-therapy four years and the degree at the health centre in Bayreuth / Germany!

Mr. Freud – Kast – Kandl – Frankl and others became very important in my psychological work.

2009 Addiction Counselor

2010 Practice of retail banking!

2014 Book "How to become an Earth-Angel" in German

2015 Translation of the German Book "Wie werde ich ein Erdenengel" in English

2015 BLOG:

ClarissaSeite.Tumblr.com

2015 book & e-book BoD

25 years later, after I bought my first card - set & after learning – reading – practices - working – studying – doing – reading and finally working, I became more and more professional over the years!

Membership at:

Organisation of Healers in Germany - (DGH)

Members of naturopath - naturopath of psychotherapy – psychotherapy of counselor - Germany - (VFP)

Clarissa.Lichtweg@gmx.de

www.theralupa.de

www.heil-verzeichnis.de

Blog:

ClarissaSeite.Tumblr.com

My staff motto is always being a teacher & student at ones ;-)

Again and again ... on the way to the master of universe – just a joke ;-)

And maybe to come back to rebirth into this world on mother earth with my old soul as an Earth-Angel again!

"The way is the goal"

[Konfuzius]

Impressum:

Umsatzsteuer-ID-Nr 82 096
358 479

Handelsregister-Nr. / Steuer-
Nr. / ggfls. Geschäftsführer

Praxis - Clarissa Mathilda Seite - Heilpraktikerin für Psycho-
therapie[HPG] - WOR

Steuernummer – Finanzamt
Wolfratshausen –
169/258/90344 – IdNr. 82 096
358 479

Bankverbindung – Sparda
Bank Nürnberg – BLZ 760 90
500 – Kontonr.: 442 50 59

[Gemäß § 4 Nr. 14 Buchst. a
UStG sind Heilbehandlungen
im Bereich der Humanmedizin
umsatzsteuerfrei. Dazu zählen
auch die Leistungen der Heil-
praktiker].

Herstellung und Verlag:
BoD - Books on Demand,
Norderstedt

ISBN 978-3-7386-5030-3

Your personal notes:

Look at exercise at page 105

Your personal notes:

Look at Exercise at page 105

Many thanks to my parents "Josef & Rosemarie Zickler, who created me with all my special sides of my character

My special sisters & brothers who showed me the way …

My best friends:

Anette / Hausen-Rhön-Germany

Bea / Hagen-Switzerland

Gitti / Bayreuth-Germany

My lovely son Frank who holds up the mirrow for me to look at! He took the pic of the front cover of this book at Gardasee / Italy / Limone! I'll tell ya …

My husband Willi & son Jonas who bring me on the edge sometimes ;-)

I love you all …

Attention Please!

The author of this book does not dispense medical advice or prescribe the use of any technique as a form of treatment for physical or medical problems without the advice of a physician, either directly or indirectly.

The intent of the author is only to offer information of a general nature to help you in your quest for emotional and spiritual well-being. In the event you use any of the information in this book for yourself which is your constitutional right, the author and the publisher assume no responsibility for your action.

I am

Happy

Healthy

&

Healed

I am …

Pretty

Lucky

Funny

Self - confident

Successful

[**Louise L. Hay**]

LOVE

IS

THE

ANSWER,

BLESS

YOU

ALL

THANK YOU A LOT!

Last but not least:

"LOVE" is the highest power in the universe.

The highest form and level of vibration / energy, which is given us from above …

"The universal power"!

Love is the answer of all questions…

Open your heart and let all the power into yours and just live the wonderful energy!

"Here & Now"

Bless you, too!

Best wishes & regards

Love & Light - Clarissa M. Seite